The Bulldog Guide to Negotiation Terms

A Dictionary of Dealmaking Principles, Strategies and Tactics

Terrance Moore, J.D.

"The Bulldog Lawyer"

Published 2025 by Bulldog Press, Minneapolis, MN

Every effort has been made to obtain permissions for material quoted throughout the book. If any required acknowledgements have been omitted, or any rights overlooked, it is unintentional. Please notify the publisher of any omission, and it will be rectified in future editions. While I am a bulldog lawyer, I am not yet *your* bulldog lawyer. Nothing in this book should be considered legal advice.

Amazon KDP Edition

ISBN: 978-1-7368906-5-3

Library of Congress Control Number: TBD

Printed in the United States

High Praise

"Terry hits the sweet spot by telling memorable stories that illustrate important principles, from someone who has lived it on the front lines."

~ John Branca, Ziffren Brittenham, LLP

"Terry is a Bulldog Lawyer: creative, strategic and ethical. This book will help businesspeople create strong partnerships."

~ George Soule, Attorney, Soule & Stull

"As a Wall Street trader, I'm used to tough negotiators. Terry's Bulldog system is the strongest I've ever seen."

~ Tad Lundborg, Private Investor

"Every deal maker should read this book. It is the difference between good deals and great results.

~ Joachim Attefjord, Commodities Trader

"Bulldog Dealmaking works whether I am buying real estate or negotiating with sub-contractors. It's as strong as any system I've ever seen."

~ Private Equity Fund Manager

Table of Contents

What Makes a Bulldog?

1. **Integrity**: Be honest with everyone, including yourself.

2. **Tenacity**: Go after what you want and don't stop until you have it.

3. **Courage**: Take on the hard challenges and big projects.

4. **Ferocity**: When you attack, attack with everything you have.

5. **Loyalty**: Be true to your allies.

6. **Pugnacity**: Never shy away from a necessary fight.

7. **Judgment**: Choose your actions deliberately.

Introduction

It's good to be a Bulldog. It's not always about compromises and smiles. A deal is not "win-win" unless you actually get what *you* want.

This book is a tactical,

The 7 Qualities That Define a Bulldog

You've seen bulldogs in the real world. They're not always loud, not always flashy. But they never let go. Bulldogs get the deal because they're willing to grind it out, stay in the game, and force a win where others would fold. That's what this book is about, building those qualities into your negotiation muscle memory.

1. Integrity

Be honest with everyone, especially yourself. That means no bluffing just to bluff, no half-truths to cover sloppy strategy. The Bulldog wins with clean lines and hard facts. You may want to inspire fear or love, whichever works in the situation, but you *always* want to inspire respect.

2. Tenacity

The Bulldog doesn't stop. When other people get tired or discouraged, the Bulldog leans in. If you're working a deal that takes eighteen months to close, the Bulldog shows up on month nineteen with the same fire as on day one. Persistence breaks resistance.

3. Courage

Courage is not the absence of fear but moving forward in the face of fear. Weak players avoid confrontation. Bulldogs do the hard things. Not for drama, but because they know that power is tested in the heat. That difficult phone call? The impossible counteroffer? The high-stakes bluff? Bulldogs choose action when others freeze.

4. Ferocity

When the time comes to strike, strike hard. Don't tap the door. Kick it open. When you have leverage, press it. When you sense weakness, exploit it. The Bulldog doesn't bite halfway. When it's time to move, move with full force.

5. Loyalty

Loyalty doesn't mean softness. It means fighting like hell for the people who back you. For your partners, your team, your clients. Loyalty builds reputation. It creates trust, and in this world, your reputation is your calling card.

6. Pugnacity

Bulldogs don't look for fights, but they always engage when it's the right thing to do. There are fights you must walk toward. Not every deal is polite. Not every opponent wants to be fair. When the time comes to throw down legally, verbally, or strategically, the

Bulldog steps up. Some deals can only be won by outfighting the other side.

7. Judgment

Judgment is what separates a Bulldog from a brawler. Every great dealmaker has to know when to push, when to pause, when to walk. It's the ability to read the room, calculate risk, and make sharp, intentional moves. You want to be dangerous, not reckless. Strategic, not stubborn.

Terms, Strategies and Tactics for Bulldog Dealmakers

These terms form the foundation of any negotiation, providing the critical concepts that all negotiators must know to understand the dynamics of the process.

Amendments/Modification Clause

n. Requires changes to be made in a specified form, typically a signed writing.

Example: This Agreement may be amended, modified, or supplemented only by a written instrument that expressly states it amends this Agreement and is signed by authorized representatives of both Parties. No oral statements or course of dealing shall modify this Agreement."

Bulldog Insight: While on its face, such a provision requires changes to the contract be made only in writing, that's not always the case. Most states have case law providing that even a contract can be modified by course of dealing or conduct of the parties, even if it contains such a provision.

Anchoring

v. Also known as Big Pot. Occurs when the first offer made sets the reference point for the negotiation, heavily influencing subsequent offers and counteroffers.

Example: A seller asks for $50,000 for a car, knowing that a reasonable price would be $40,000. The initial asking price serves as the anchor.

Bulldog Insight: The initial anchor is intended to influence the direction of the negotiation and may not be representative of the final outcome. Strong anchors can allow you to secure a deal closer to your ideal terms. Weak, or unjustified anchors hurt your credibility.

Assignment Clause

The Assignment Clause controls whether rights or obligations may be transferred to another person or entity. If it's assignable, the clause will control how an assignment is made.

Examples:

Not assignable: Neither Party may assign, delegate, or otherwise transfer this Agreement, in whole or in part, by operation of law or otherwise, without the prior written consent of the other Party. Any purported transfer in violation of this Section is void.

Assignable with qualifications: Neither Party may assign this Agreement without the prior written consent of the other Party, which consent shall not be unreasonably withheld, conditioned, or delayed; provided, however, either Party may assign this Agreement without consent to (a) an Affiliate or (b) a successor in connection with a transfer of substantially all of its assets or voting securities upon written notice.

Fully Assignable: Either Party may assign or transfer this Agreement, in whole or in part, upon written notice to the other Party. Any assignee shall assume all obligations under this Agreement

Bulldog Insight: Assignment clauses deal with future rights, so are often given little value up front. You can add value to your side by understanding your future plans and shaping the provision accordingly.

BATNA

n. Best Alternative To a Negotiated Agreement. BATNA is your backup plan if negotiations fail. It's the best option available to you if negotiations fail.

Example: While negotiating the sale of your car with an interested buyer, you receive another offer for $18,000. If the current deal doesn't work out, your BATNA is accepting the $18,000 from the other buyer.

Bulldog Insight: The relative strength of the parties' BATNAs determines leverage. BATNA is crucial for determining whether a negotiated agreement is worth pursuing. Knowing both your and the other party's BATNA is critical to determining your negotiation strategy.

If you do not like your BATNA, you can change it. Bring in new players (like another buyer), eliminate or diminish the opposition's BATNA, or find another way to increase your leverage.

Big Pot

n. In the Big Pot tactic, a negotiator starts with a large number of demands, some real and some fabricated, to create the perception of a complex negotiation. Then, the proponent claims to be reasonable because of his many concessions.

Example: A job candidate wants a high salary, so they ask for the high salary, plus more PTO, a better parking spot, a signing bonus and more work from home time.

Bulldog Insight: Big Pot can be an effective tactic. It can also backfire when they agree to give you the parking spot but not the salary. If you see someone using the Big Pot, a good response can be giving away what you do not care about and sticking hard on the issues you do care about.

Bluffing

v. Involves presenting a position or threat that is not true, hoping to manipulate the other party into making concessions or agreeing to terms.

Example: A negotiator claims they have another buyer ready with a higher offer for a property, even though no such offer exists.

Bulldog Insight: Bluffing can be effective when the other party doesn't challenge it but will backfire if revealed. It's a risky tactic and can damage trust in the long run. I prefer straightforward communication and generally avoid bluffing.

Body Language

n. Non-verbal cues that convey messages about a negotiator's true feelings, intentions, or level of interest.

Example: A negotiator leaning forward during a discussion might indicate interest or eagerness, while crossing their arms and leaning back may signal defensiveness or disinterest.

Bulldog Insight: Awareness of body language can help a negotiator read the other party's emotions and intentions. Misreading body language can lead to misunderstandings. Practice reading body language whenever you're in a public place.

Some basic body language clues:

- Open arms means open to the idea.
- Closed arms or crossed legs mean closed to the communication.
- If sitting, knees facing the speaker indicates interest and knees facing away shows disinterest.
- A speaker who puts his hand or finger in front of his mouth does not believe what he's saying.
- Touching your nose indicates disgust with the conversation and is also a sign of giving up.

Buying Signals

n. Any verbal or non-verbal indication that the other party is ready to move forward to the next step in the process.

Example: A buyer says, “What are the payment terms?” This is a buying signal, suggesting they’ve decided they want the product and are ready to buy at the right price.

Bulldog Insight: Recognizing buying signals helps you move the negotiation towards closure. Be attuned to both spoken words and body language for more subtle buying signals. Whenever you see a buying signal, move the conversation a level closer to closing.

Closing Tactics

n. Techniques used to push a negotiation toward final agreement, often by emphasizing urgency or sweetening the deal.

Example: In the False Withdrawal Close, a buyer might say, "This deal is not going to work for me," and start packing up as if to leave. The seller, fearing they will lose the sale, may offer a better price to keep the buyer engaged.

Bulldog Insight: Closing tactics create pressure to make a decision. These tactics are essential to reaching final agreement and must be carefully chosen to match the situation and relationship. When closing, you want to create urgency, scarcity or another situation that makes accepting your proposal more attractive to your opponent than continuing to negotiate.

Closing the Deal

v. The end game in the negotiation where you take the final actions necessary to bring your opponent to agreement.

Example: "It looks like we've covered everything that matters to you — timing, price, and support. If you're comfortable with what we've outlined, I can send over the agreement today so we can get started."

Bulldog Insight: Unless you can close, negotiations are a waste of time. Motivating your opponent to agree with you requires choosing closing tactics that motivate your opponent, which can include creating either positive or negative pressure on your opponent.

Commitment

n. The degree to which a party is tied to their position. It can be a positive tool to indicate firmness, or it can be a weakness if not handled strategically.

Example: A seller commits to a price based on market conditions, making it clear they're not willing to negotiate further, which pressures the buyer to decide whether to agree or walk away. In the movie "True Grit," the horse trader says, "That's my bottom line, you can take it or leave it and I don't much care what you decide."

Bulldog Insight: Clear commitment creates leverage by increasing credibility and fixing expectations. Committing too early may limit flexibility, particularly if market conditions or new information arise.

Concessions

n. Compromises or adjustments one party makes to their original offer in response to the other party's needs or demands.

Example: "We're both aiming for a long-term relationship, not just a transaction. I'm willing to give a little here so we start on the right foot. I can get this deal done at $250,000."

Bulldog Insight: Concessions should be made strategically to avoid giving away too much without gaining value in return. Each concession should be planned and have a purpose within your overall strategy.

Confidentiality/Non-Disclosure

n. Obligates parties to protect specified information and limit its use or disclosure.

Example: Each Party agrees to keep confidential and not disclose to any third party any non-public information received from the other Party in connection with this Agreement ("Confidential Information"). Each Party shall use such Confidential Information solely for the purpose of evaluating, negotiating, or performing this Agreement. The obligations of confidentiality shall not apply to information that (a) is or becomes public through no fault of the receiving Party; (b) is rightfully received from a third party without restriction; or (c) is independently developed without use of the Confidential Information. These obligations shall remain in effect for three (3) years following the termination of this Agreement.

Bulldog Insight: At its core, a confidentiality clause is a promise not to disclose or misuse information shared during a negotiation, business relationship, or settlement. Its main purpose is to serve as a deterrent to disclosure of your confidential information. A well-drafted clause has teeth, often in the form of the right to seek injunctions or damages if the promise is broken. Even the existence of that clause can deter leaks because the other side knows it's enforceable.

Counterparts/Electronic Signatures

n. Permits signing in separate copies and via electronic means, each treated as an original.

Example: "This Agreement may be executed in counterparts and by electronic signature, each of which shall be deemed an original."

Bulldog Insight: Except in residential real estate, the old-fashioned closing around a conference room table is rarely used anymore. Permitting signatures in counterparts or electronically is makes contract execution faster, more practical, and legally secure in modern business. This is a standard contract clause.

Deal Range

n. The range of acceptable terms, where the seller's minimum and the buyer's maximum intersect, defining the range within which a deal can be reached.

Example: In a real estate deal, Bob Buyer is willing to pay up to $300,000, while Sam Seller will accept no less than $280,000. The Deal Range is now between $280,000 and $300,000. The final price will fall within this range.

Bulldog Insight: The deal range is fluid and can shift as parties adjust their expectations. Understanding the deal range helps you develop a strategic plan to reach agreement at your favorable end of the range.

Decoy Effect

n. occurs when a less attractive option is introduced to make another option seem more attractive by comparison.

Example: A restaurant offers three pricing tiers for a wine selection: $20, $50, and $75. The $50 bottle is a decoy that makes the $75 bottle seem like a good deal.

Bulldog Insight: The decoy effect can influence choices by changing the way options are perceived. It's often used in marketing but can also be applied in negotiations. A Big Pot proposal is an example of the Decoy Effect.

Definitions Clause

n. Gives precise meanings to capitalized terms to avoid ambiguity elsewhere in the contract.

Example: A contract that says, "Payment is due within five (5) Business Days," might define "Business Day" as any day other than a Saturday, Sunday, or federal holiday removes argument over timing.

Bulldog Insight: Definitions ensure that the parties' intent is clear in the contract. If a contract is ambiguous, two honest parties can misunderstand the meaning of an important clause, thus giving rise to litigation. A Definitions section also makes contracts less cumbersome, enabling the parties to say "Business Day" six times instead of saying "any day other than a Saturday, Sunday, or federal holiday" removes the ambiguity over timing six times.

Dispute Resolution

n. Specifies whether disputes go to mediation, arbitration, or court and may dictate the rules for dispute resolution.

Example: "Any disputes under this contract shall be resolved by binding arbitration in New York, NY."

Bulldog Insight: The fundamental purpose of a dispute resolution provision is to create certainty about the process for resolving disputes. Without this clause, parties may fight later about where to sue, what law applies, and how disputes should be handled. That uncertainty is expensive, time-consuming, and can itself become a tactical weapon.

Emotional Intelligence

n. (EI) The ability to understand and manage your emotions, as well as recognize and influence the emotions of others. EI enhances communication and decision-making.

Example: Sally Seller is negotiating the sale of her company to a larger competitor. After weeks of talks, the buyer's CFO says in a tense meeting: "Your valuation expectations are unrealistic. We've already stretched beyond our limits."

Instead of reacting defensively ("You don't understand the business!"), Sally takes a breath. She recognizes her own frustration but also understands the buyer's perception that he understands the industry better than her.

So she pauses and calmly replies: "I hear that you feel the valuation is high. Let's talk through what's driving that feeling."

Bulldog Insight: Emotional Intelligence (EI) is one of the most underrated yet decisive factors in successful negotiation.

You should develop your EI. High EI enables better rapport-building and conflict resolution. By understanding your opponent's emotions, you can inform your strategy to better motivate them to agree. EI helps in maintaining control over your own emotions and managing difficult negotiations.

Entire Agreement/Integration Clause

n. Confirms the written contract is the complete deal, superseding prior communications. Also known as a Merger Clause

Example: This Agreement constitutes the entire understanding between the Parties with respect to the subject matter hereof and supersedes all prior and contemporaneous agreements, negotiations, representations, and understandings, whether oral or written, relating to such subject matter.

Bulldog Insight: A merger clause tells everyone, including a future judge or jury, that this contract contains the whole deal, and nothing else counts. It prevents either party from later claiming that there was an oral promise or that emails, conversations, or marketing statements formed part of the contract.

In short, it locks the parties into only what's written in the final signed agreement. Most agreements contain this clause, so if you want something in the agreement, you had better make sure it's in there.

Evergreen Renewal

n. Automatically renews the contract for additional periods unless timely notice of non-renewal is given.

Example: This Agreement shall have an initial term of one (1) year and shall automatically renew for successive one (1) year periods unless either Party provides written notice of its intent not to renew at least thirty (30) days prior to the expiration of the then-current term.

Bulldog Insight: Negotiating renewals takes time, attention, and often legal fees. Evergreen clauses save effort by letting a contract quietly continue unless someone wants to change it. An evergreen renewal clause ensures that a contract continues automatically unless someone takes action to terminate it.

When renewal is the default, the contract will continue on its own unless one party raises an issue.

Face-saving

v. The act of preserving the other party's dignity or avoiding embarrassment during negotiations. Nobody wants to be embarrassed, so when you're getting a big win, closing the deal may require concession that allow the other side to save face.

Example: I had a case where two people had been in a relationship off and on for twenty years and had three children. They never married. My client had inherited a ranch that turned out to contain mineral deposits worth millions. When he ended the relationship for good, she sued for common law marriage and half of his assets. She had no case because the state where they lived doesn't recognize common law marriage. In order to settle the case, we let her have a small house, gave her $100,000 to get on her feet and put money in trust for their children. Had we insisted on giving her nothing, we could not have reached an agreement because she had nothing to lose.

Bulldog Insight: Face-saving is particularly important in negotiations where you have all the leverage. To motivate the other side to make a deal, concede something slightly better than their BATNA. By making your offer better than their BATNA, they have something to lose and will take the deal.

Fairness Norm

n. The expectation that both sides in a negotiation will act with fairness, providing a balanced and equitable deal. When one side perceives that the other is being unfair, the negotiation may break down.

Example: In a business contract negotiation, both parties expect to share profits in a way that reflects their contributions,

Bulldog Insight: Nobody really cares about "fairness" until they feel they've been treated unfairly. Fairness is a sign of respect and should usually be maintained in long-term relationships and trust-dependent relationships. In high-leverage situations, fairness is often a non-factor.

False Withdrawal

n. A closing tactic where a negotiator threatens to walk away from the deal to make the other party reconsider their position or offer better terms.

Example: During a price negotiation, a buyer might say, "This deal is not going to work for me," and start packing up as if to leave. The seller, fearing they will lose the sale, may offer a better price to keep the buyer engaged.

Bulldog Insight: False withdrawals can prompt a counteroffer, but they may also diminish credibility if the tactic is overused. It is most effective when the other party has a weak BATNA or he incurs a significant cost if you leave the deal.

The False Withdrawal works by creating remorse in the other party when he believes the negotiations have broken down.

Final Offer

n. A tactic where one side declares that their current offer is the best they can provide, suggesting that no further negotiation is possible. This can often encourage the other party to either accept the deal or walk away.

Example: Mike Manufacturer says, "We've already extended our pricing, adjusted delivery, and met your main conditions. This proposal reflects all of those concessions — it's our final offer. If you can commit to signing by Friday, we can honor these terms."

Bulldog Insight: Never state that your offer is final unless it is. This tactic is used to create urgency when you are at the far end of your Deal Range. You can also use it when you have high leverage or a strong BATNA.

First Response

n. This is your response to the other party's first offer. It sets the tone for the rest of the negotiation.

Example: In response to an opening offer of $30,000, Pam Plaintiff might immediately counter with $45,000, establishing a higher starting point for the negotiation. Or she could give them the Golden Silence, or a straight rejection.

Bulldog Insight: The first response influences the direction of the negotiation and shapes future interactions. Timing and tone are crucial. Making an impulsive or emotional first response can weaken your position. Be prepared ahead of time so you know how you will respond to each potential proposal from the other side.

Force Majeure

n. Excuses performance when extraordinary events beyond the parties' control prevent or delay obligations.

Example: Neither Party shall be liable for any failure or delay in performance under this Agreement (other than payment obligations) to the extent caused by circumstances beyond its reasonable control, including acts of God, natural disasters, war, terrorism, civil unrest, labor disputes, epidemics, governmental actions, or interruptions of utilities or transportation. The affected Party shall promptly notify the other Party of the event and use reasonable efforts to resume performance as soon as practicable.

Bulldog Insight: A force majeure clause decides who bears the loss when extraordinary events occur — things like natural disasters, wars, pandemics, or government shutdowns. Without the clause, a party who fails to perform could be found in breach of contract, even if the failure wasn't their fault.

With the clause, the risk is shared or excused, allowing performance to be delayed or suspended instead of punished.

Framing

v. How information is presented in negotiations, influencing how the other party perceives the deal or proposal.

Example: A seller might present a product's price as a "discount" from the original price, framing the deal in a positive light making it appear to be a better value.

Bulldog Insight: Use framing to influence perception, making a bad deal look better or a good deal seem essential. It's important to plan how your offers are framed and anticipate how the other party may reframe your proposals.

Golden Silence

v. Remaining quiet after a proposal or counteroffer is made, forcing the other party to fill the silence. This often leads them to make concessions or provide more information.

Example: After weeks of talks, the buyer's representative says, "We could probably make this work at $1.8 million." You know your target price is $2 million — but instead of countering, explaining, or arguing, you simply wait to respond. Depending on the situation, The Golden Silence might last for minutes, days or even weeks.

Bulldog Insight: Using silence creates discomfort and prompts better proposals. Most people feel compelled to fill the silence. The tactic works best when you remain calm and composed during the silence.

Good Cop/Bad Cop

n. A tactic where one negotiator on your team takes a tough, unyielding position (the "bad cop") while the other plays a more conciliatory, agreeable role (the "good cop") to create pressure on the other party to agree.

Example: In a salary negotiation, one manager might offer an employee a minimal raise, pointing out all the bad things in his file. Then another manager steps in and offers praise and a slightly more generous raise. This leads the employee to be grateful for the increased offer and more likely to accept it.

Bulldog Insight: Avoid this tactic because it's overused, and often transparent. When facing Good Cop/Bad Cop, exclude the bad cop and communicate only with the good cop. It also may help to call out the strategy, which will defuse it.

A more subtle version of this tactic is to extend it to the entire negotiation process. One team member always speaks when your team is acting cooperatively and the other always speaks when your team is being uncooperative. During the end game, your final proposal will be received better if the good cop delivers it.

Governing Law

n. Identifies the jurisdiction's law that will interpret and apply to the contract and where litigation will take place.

Example: This Agreement shall be governed by and construed in accordance with the laws of the State of New York, without regard to conflict of law principles. Any legal action or proceeding arising out of or relating to this Agreement shall be brought exclusively in the state or federal courts located in New York County, New York, and each Party hereby irrevocably submits to the jurisdiction of such courts.

Bulldog Insight: By determining which state's law will govern the contract, you are deciding the rules that will apply to any dispute, and that will often determine who wins! Also, it's far less expensive to litigate in your home state than one far away. Make sure you understand how the chosen governing law affects important contract provisions.

Hidden Concessions

n. Subtle or unspoken signals that indicate that the other side is willing to compromise on a deal point. Hidden Concessions are often not immediately apparent. These concessions can be accidental, but they are real.

Example: When Bety Buyer says "I only have authority to offer you $500,000," the hidden concession is that she *will* be able to go back and get authority to pay more. "I will never pay $300,000," usually means that, in fact, he *will* pay $300,000. "Points 1, 3, and 5 are important to us," means they have flexibility on points 2 and 4.

Bulldog Insight: Hidden concessions are real. When you hear one, you should incorporate it into your strategy. As often as not, you can solidify a hidden concession by asking about it directly. "So, you have some flexibility on points 2 and 4?" or, "If you only have authority to offer $500,000, is this a take-it-or-leave-it offer?"

Highball/Lowball Proposal

v. Anchoring tactics where one party makes an extreme initial offer—either much higher or lower than what they expect to settle for—to set the stage for negotiation.

Example: Anne the business owner offers to buy a competitor's company for $500,000, even though both sides know it's worth closer to $1 million. When Carl Competitor continues the talks (instead of walking away) Anne knows he's motivated to sell. Anne says, "I understand that's less than you expected, but given the risk and the investment we'll need to make, that's where we need to be to make this viable." When she later raises the offer to $700,000, it seems fair even though it's still below market value.

Bulldog Insight: This tactic is effective when you have high leverage. Beware, because it can backfire if the initial offer is too extreme. Be ready to justify your position.

Indemnification

n. Requires one party to defend and reimburse the other for losses from specified claims or breaches. If one party causes harm to a third party, they agree to protect the other from lawsuits or costs from that third party.

Example: Each Party ("Indemnifying Party") shall indemnify, defend, and hold harmless the other Party, its officers, directors, employees, and agents ("Indemnified Party") from and against any and all claims, damages, liabilities, losses, costs, and expenses (including reasonable attorneys' fees) arising out of or relating to any third-party claim resulting from the Indemnifying Party's (a) breach of this Agreement, (b) negligence, or (c) willful misconduct.

Bulldog Insight: Most contracts have mutual indemnity clauses. When they have high leverage, Bulldog dealmakers will seek a one-way indemnity clause in their favor. You should almost never agree to a one-way clause where you have an indemnity obligation and the other side does not.

Integrative Negotiation

n. A type of negotiation where both parties collaborate to find a mutually beneficial solution. The goal is to expand the pie, rather than divide it, creating more value for both sides.

Example: Two companies negotiating a supply contract might agree to share logistics resources, which reduces costs for both and improves efficiency, creating more value than simply negotiating price alone.

Bulldog Insight: This approach promotes long-term relationships and builds trust. It requires creativity and an open mindset to explore options that satisfy both parties' interests.

Inventions Clause

n. Allocates ownership and usage rights for Intellectual Property (IP including copyrights, patents, trademarks, or trade secrets) used or created under the agreement. Decides who owns creative work, inventions, or ideas made during the term of the contract and beyond.

Example: Employee agrees that all inventions, discoveries, designs, developments, improvements, processes, software, and works of authorship (collectively, "Inventions") that Employee conceives, creates, or reduces to practice, alone or jointly with others, during the term of employment and relating to the Company's business or anticipated research shall be the sole property of the Company. Employee hereby assigns to the Company all rights, title, and interest in such Inventions and agrees to execute any documents necessary to confirm such ownership.

Bulldog Insight: Intellectual property can be extremely valuable, but it's often overlooked. The main reason for including an inventions clause is to ensure that the company, not the employee, owns the intellectual property created using its time, tools, and resources.

When a company contracts with an outside firm to develop software or other product, and the company maintains ownership of all intellectual property created by that firm, it's called a Work For Hire contract.

Jurisdiction and Venue Clause

n. Designates the forum and geographical location where disputes must be resolved.

Example: The Parties agree that any legal action or proceeding arising out of or relating to this Agreement shall be brought exclusively in the state or federal courts located in Hennepin County, Minnesota, and each Party hereby irrevocably submits to the personal jurisdiction of such courts. The Parties waive any objection to venue or claim that such courts are an inconvenient forum.

Bulldog Insight: The advantage of setting the jurisdiction and venue in your home town is that you will be able to fight on your own turf. You (and your lawyer) know the local laws, judges, and procedural rules. You can easily and inexpensively attend hearings, depositions, and meetings, while your opposition must travel, which raises their cost and inconvenience. Every small friction — travel time, cost, unfamiliarity — pushes the other side toward compromise or settlement.

Of course, many large companies insist on using their home jurisdiction. The remote possibility of further dispute, plus the lack of value at the outset, means that you will sometimes concede to the other side's position on jurisdiction and venue.

Leverage

n. The ability to influence or control the negotiation process. It's typically based on the strength of your position, including BATNA, relative to the other players.

Example: If you're the only supplier of a critical component, you hold leverage in negotiations with your buyer.

Bulldog Insight: The more leverage you have, the more power you hold in dictating the terms of the deal.

Leverage is determined by the relative BATNAs of the parties. A high-leverage situation in negotiation is one where one side has a much stronger BATNA than the other.

Leverage is firm, but not static. You can change it by changing the BATNA of either side.

Limitation of Liability Clause

n. Caps the types and amounts of damages recoverable under the agreement.

Example: Except for liability arising from gross negligence, willful misconduct, or breach of confidentiality, neither Party shall be liable to the other for any indirect, incidental, consequential, special, or punitive damages, including lost profits or loss of data, even if advised of the possibility of such damages. Each Party's total cumulative liability under this Agreement shall not exceed the total amount of fees paid by Client to Company under this Agreement during the twelve (12) months preceding the event giving rise to the claim.

Bulldog Insight: The purpose of a Limitation of Liability Clause is to cap or restrict how much one party can be held financially responsible for if something goes wrong, such as a breach, mistake, or loss. They protect businesses from catastrophic exposure and make risk more predictable and thus more insurable.

Mutual Gains Approach

n. A focus on creating value for both parties by identifying shared interests and finding solutions that benefit everyone involved. *See also* Win-Win.

Example: In a labor negotiation, the union and management agree to improved working conditions, which benefits management by making employees more productive and the union because the employees have a better place to work.

Bulldog Insight: The Mutual Gains Approach is used in Win-Win games. This approach supports long-term relationships by fostering trust, respect, and goodwill between the parties. The key to the Mutual Gains Approach is to grow the pie so that both sides benefit. It can be useful in situations where leverage is balanced or when you have low leverage.

Narrowing the Range

v. A negotiation tactic where one party aims to reduce the gap between their offer and the other party's expectations, often by making small adjustments or offering creative solutions.

Example: Sarah Seller is asking for $110,000 for her classic car. Billy Buyer has offered $75,000. Sarah says, "I can come off my $110,000, but we both know $75,000 is too low. I can come down to $100 if you can come up to $85."

Bulldog Insight: Bulldogs narrow the range to make it easier to reach a mutually acceptable agreement. This tactic can be effective when the parties are close to agreement but stalling out. The example above employs the Bracketing technique. If Billy agrees, then the range is narrowed to between $85 and $100, much closer than before. Sarah has narrowed the range.

Nibbling

v. Asking for small, additional concessions, at or near the end of a negotiation, often catching the other party off guard.

Example: After agreeing on the price of a car, Carla Customer asks for a free set of floor mats, a free oil change, or other small extras, knowing that Don Dealer is likely to provide these low-cost items to close the sale.

Bulldog Insight: Nibbling can add significant value if the other party is emotionally committed to the deal. It should be done carefully, as it can irritate the other party if it's seen as exploiting their desire to conclude. If you face a nibbler, you should only concede the *first* nibble *after* clarifying that if you do so, the deal is complete.

Non-Circumvention Clause

n. Prevents a party from bypassing the other to deal directly with introduced clients or contacts.

Example: During the term of this Agreement and for two (2) years thereafter, neither party shall circumvent the other by directly or indirectly contacting, soliciting, or conducting business with the other party's clients, suppliers, or contacts disclosed under this Agreement without prior written consent.

Bulldog Insight: This clause protects the value of your business relationships. If you introduce a supplier, customer, or investor to the other side, they can't go around you and strike their own deal behind your back. It preserves trust, ensures you're compensated for making introductions, and prevents your strategic contacts from being poached.

Non-Compete

n. Restricts a party from engaging in competing activities during and/or after the term.

Example: Contractor shall not compete with Company's business for one year after termination.

Bulldog Insight: Non-compete laws vary widely from state to state, and some states do not recognize them as valid. Make sure you know the law of the state that governs. An employer will argue that every employee who regularly faces customers or suppliers should have a non-compete. An employee will argue that the clause is designed to impair their ability to make a living, effectively chaining them to the employer.

Non-Disclosure/Confidentiality*

n. Obligates parties to protect specified information and limit its use or disclosure.

Example: Each Party agrees to keep confidential and not disclose to any third party any non-public information received from the other Party in connection with this Agreement ("Confidential Information"). Each Party shall use such Confidential Information solely for the purpose of evaluating, negotiating, or performing this Agreement. The obligations of confidentiality shall not apply to information that (a) is or becomes public through no fault of the receiving Party; (b) is rightfully received from a third party without restriction; or (c) is independently developed without use of the Confidential Information. These obligations shall remain in effect for three (3) years following the termination of this Agreement.

Bulldog Insight: At its core, a confidentiality clause is a promise not to disclose or misuse information shared during a negotiation, business relationship, or settlement. It's main purpose is to serve as a deterrent to disclosure of your confidential information. A well-drafted clause has teeth, often in the form of the right to seek injunctions or damages if the promise is broken. Even the existence of that clause can deter leaks because the other side knows it's enforceable.

Non-Solicitation

n. Prohibits soliciting or hiring the other party's employees, contractors, or customers for a period of time.

Example: The Seller agrees that for the term of this agreement, and for two years after its termination date, neither the Seller nor any of its affiliates shall, directly or indirectly: (a) Solicit, induce, or attempt to induce any employee or independent contractor of the Buyer to terminate their relationship with the Buyer; or (b) Solicit or attempt to solicit any customer, supplier, or business partner of the Buyer for purposes of providing goods or services competitive with the Buyer's business.

Bulldog Insight: The most significant benefit of a non-solicitation clause is that it safeguards the company's customer base, employees and goodwill. As a practical matter, certain employees often have stronger relationships with customers than the owners have. A non-solicitation provision in an employment contract prevents the employee form poaching customers. Likewise, a non-solicitation provision in a company-customer contract prevents the customer from hiring away the employee.

Notice Provision

n. Dictates how and where formal notices must be delivered for them to be effective.

Example: Any notice required or permitted to be given under this Agreement shall be in writing and shall be deemed duly given when: (a) delivered personally, (b) sent by certified or registered mail, return receipt requested, postage prepaid, or (c) sent by a nationally recognized overnight courier service to the addresses set forth below (or to such other address as a party may designate by written notice). Notices shall be deemed effective on the date of delivery if personally delivered or sent by courier, and three (3) business days after mailing if sent by certified mail.

Addresses for Notice:

If to Sheriff: ____________________

If to Robin Hood:________________

Bulldog Insight: The primary purpose of a notice provision is to eliminate ambiguity about whether a party properly gave notice. Without one, parties will argue about whether an email or phone call provided official notice.

This clarity avoids misunderstanding (and often litigation) about whether notice was properly given.

Package Deal

v. Bundling multiple issues or items together, allowing the negotiators to reach an agreement on the entire package rather than negotiating each element separately.

Example: Vicky Vendor offers a package deal for software that includes installation, maintenance, and training, rather than selling each service separately. By doing so, she creates better pricing for her customers.

Bulldog Insight: Package deals are effective in creating a win-win scenario, where both sides feel they are receiving value. The seller increases the deal size and the buyer gets value at reduced cost. They can also simplify negotiations by reducing the number of items being negotiated separately.

Parties Clause

n. Names the legal entities bound by the agreement and how they will be referred to throughout.

Example: This Agreement ("Agreement") is made and entered into as of [Date], by and between ABC Holdings, LLC, a Delaware limited liability company with its principal place of business at 123 Main Street, Wilmington, DE 19801 ("Company"), and IDK LLC., a California corporation with its principal place of business at 1313 Mickingbird Lane, San Francisco, CA 94105 ("Consultant"). The Company and the Consultant are each referred to herein individually as a "Party" and collectively as the "Parties."

Bulldog Insight: Identifies who the contract is between. You need to know exactly who is bound.

Bulldog Insight: Be careful to use the proper names of parties. If the named party is misidentified, you may not be able to enforce your contractual rights. If you are not sure of the other side's proper name, ask them in writing to provide it to you, then look them up to make sure you are dealing with the right party.

Payment Terms

n. Covers price, invoicing, timing, method of payment, and any pre-conditions to payment.

Example: The Client shall pay the Contractor a total fee of $25,000 for the services described in this Agreement. Unless otherwise agreed in writing, payment shall be made as follows: fifty percent (50%) upon execution of this Agreement and fifty percent (50%) upon completion of the services to the Client's reasonable satisfaction.

All payments shall be made in U.S. dollars by check, ACH transfer, or wire to the account designated by the Contractor.

Bulldog Insight: Payment terms are among the most critical clauses in any contract because they define the economic backbone of the deal: how, when, and under what conditions money changes hands. A contract without clear payment terms invites misunderstanding.

This clause can be negotiated to your advantage. You can grant a better payment term in exchange for more money (or the opposite). As payer, ask to pay less up front or offer a better price for more paid up front.

Post-Negotiation Evaluation

v. Reflecting on the negotiation process to assess what went well, what could be improved, and how future negotiations can be handled better.

Example: After closing a contract, a team discusses whether the terms of the deal were favorable. Where did you make mistakes or miss opportunities? What did you do well?

Bulldog Insight: Post-negotiation evaluation is vital for continuous improvement in negotiation skills. Discerning which tactics worked well and which did not helps you get better deals in the future. It helps identify your strengths and weaknesses in both tactics and strategy.

Posturing

v. A form of bluffing where you present your opposition in an exaggerated or overly firm manner to influence the other party's perceptions and decisions. It's often used to create the impression of strength or intransigence, with the goal of gaining leverage.

Example: A negotiator might say, "My Board doesn't want me to sell at this price. I doubt they will approve anything lower," even though they may be willing to make concessions later.

Bulldog Insight: Bulldogs use posturing to gain psychological leverage by creating an impression of strong resolve. Posturing signals strength and may create insecurity in your opponent. Like any bluff, posturing can backfire, making the other party feel alienated or distrustful. Avoid posturing except in low leverage situations.

Recitals Clause

n. States background facts and intent; usually binding context that can guide interpretation.

Example: WHEREAS, the Seller owns and operates a manufacturing business known as Blue Ridge Plastics (the "Business");

WHEREAS, the Buyer desires to purchase from the Seller, and the Seller desires to sell to the Buyer, substantially all of the assets, properties, and goodwill of the Business; and

WHEREAS, the Parties desire to set forth the terms and conditions of such sale and purchase in this Agreement;

NOW, THEREFORE, in consideration of the mutual covenants and agreements contained herein, the Parties agree as follows.

Bulldog Insight: Although generally non-controversial, be sure you are comfortable the Recitals Clause, because it will be used in interpretation of the contract. Disputing the Recitals Clause will signal to your opponent that you are using an aggressive strategy.

Relationship Building

v. Building rapport and trust with the other party to facilitate better understanding, reduce resistance, and achieve a win-win outcome.

Example: In a business negotiation, spending time getting to know the client's needs and concerns helps build a foundation for trust and long-term collaboration.

Bulldog Insight: Relationship building is important for long-term partnerships and success. Trust and goodwill are often as important as the terms of the deal itself. A buyer who trusts a seller's representations won't demand dozens of warranties and inspections, saving time and expense for both sides. When parties have rapport, they're more candid about priorities, risks, and flexibility. That transparency allows creative deal structures that might not emerge in a more adversarial setting.

Reservation Price

n. The maximum or minimum price a party is willing to accept within the negotiation process.

Example: A consignment seller's reservation price is $100,000. He will not sell for less. So if no offers come in at that level, he doesn't sell the piece.

Bulldog Insight: Setting a reservation price is critical. Without it, you negotiate blind, driven by emotion, pressure, or guesswork rather than strategy. Your reservation price is similar to your Walkaway Number. Depending on the negotiation context, a reservation price can be flexed. A walkaway number should not.

Scarcity

n. The tactic of making a product or opportunity appear more limited or rare, increasing its perceived value.

Example: When you look at flight prices on an airline website, you often see a notation like, "Only 3 tickets left at this price." The airline is creating scarcity to entice you to buy *right now*. Another example is when your opponent tells you that he has another interested party, or that this is the last car he has in that color.

Bulldog Insight: Fear of loss is a strong emotion. Scarcity tactics create more value for you based on the law of supply and demand. When you create scarcity, you are informing your opponent that supply is down, which drives value up.

Scarcity tactics should only be used when the scarcity is genuine. If you bluff scarcity and get called out, your value decreases. When faced with scarcity tactics, consider using the Golden Silence. You may find the deal is still there when you begin talking again.

Scope of Work/Services

n. Specifies the tasks, deliverables, and performance standards the provider must meet.

Example: The Consultant shall provide professional consulting services to the Client related to the development and implementation of the Client's strategic marketing plan (the "Services"). Specifically, the Consultant shall:

1. Conduct a market analysis and competitor benchmarking study;
2. Develop a written strategic marketing plan, including budget projections and key performance indicators; and
3. Deliver one (1) in-person presentation summarizing findings and recommendations; and

All Services shall be completed in accordance with the timeline set forth in Exhibit A. Any additional services beyond this scope must be authorized in writing by the Client and may be subject to additional fees.

Bulldog Insight: A clear Scope of Work (SOW) defines exactly what work will be performed. Providers will be held to perform the work as described. Payers will get nothing more than what is in the SOW. When the SOW is vague or incomplete, misunderstandings, scope creep, and disputes are almost guaranteed.

Seasoning

v. A tactic used when an opponent has made an offer near the low end of the Deal Range. The negotiator will downplay the attractiveness of the initial offer to make the other party desire the deal more, pushing them to make a better final offer.

Example: In a job negotiation, Ed Employer offers a salary. Although Carla Candidate likes the salary, she does not respond immediately but says she must talk to her husband. Upon return, she can tell them she is happy with the salary but has concerns that the offer doesn't meet all her needs, such as concerns about benefits or work-life balance, creating a sense of scarcity or urgency around the offer. The idea is to not agree too easily, such that the Employer gets buyer's remorse.

Bulldog Insight: You must do the whole dance. Use seasoning to help your opponent feel like they won. It can create the perception of an offer being more valuable as the negotiation progresses. If you move towards the other side without seasoning them, you may seem too motivated to get the deal done, and a strong negotiator will exploit your motivation.

Severability

n. Keeps the rest of the contract enforceable if one clause is invalid or unenforceable.

Example: If any provision of this Agreement is held to be invalid, illegal, or unenforceable by a court of competent jurisdiction, the remaining provisions shall continue in full force and effect. The Parties agree that such invalid or unenforceable provision shall be modified to the minimum extent necessary to make it valid and enforceable, consistent with the Parties' original intent.

Bulldog Insight: A severability clause is a safeguard ensuring that if one part of a contract is found to be invalid, illegal, or unenforceable, the whole agreement does not go out the window. In other words, it prevents a small legal flaw from destroying the entire deal. Every complicated contract should include a severability clause.

Sweeteners

n. The counterpart to Nibbling, Sweeteners are additional offers made to close a deal, typically added near the end of a negotiation, designed to make the overall deal more attractive.

Example: When Bart Buyer has given buying signals but is slow to commit to the purchase, Chris Cardealer offers free oil changes for a year as a sweetener to close the sale.

Bulldog Insight: Sweeteners help overcome final objections and can serve as a persuasive tool to close the deal. You can use the Nibbling tactic to obtain sweeteners near the end of the negotiations.

Take-it-or-Leave-it

n. A closing tactic where one party presents a final offer with no room for negotiation, forcing the other party to accept or reject it.

Example: Harry Haggler tells a customer, "This is the best price we can offer, take it or leave it." The customer has no opportunity to negotiate further.

Bulldog Insight: Take-it-or-Leave-it offers create pressure, but may also alienate the other party if they feel boxed in. I never tell my opponent that a proposal is take-it-or-leave-it unless it's true. It's most effective when you know your offer is a good one or when the other party has a very weak BATNA. It can also be used to close the deal when the other party is having trouble making a decision. Of note, some negotiators will never agree until you make it clear that you will not be offering anything better.

Term

n. Sets the agreement's duration—when obligations begin and when they end.

Example: This Agreement shall commence on January 1, 2025 (the "Effective Date") and shall remain in full force and effect until December 31, 2025, unless earlier terminated in accordance with the provisions of this Agreement. Upon expiration, this Agreement shall automatically terminate unless the Parties mutually agree in writing to renew or extend it.

Bulldog Insight: A clear term prevents disputes about whether the parties are still bound or free to walk away. You can negotiate a shorter or longer term in exchange for better pricing. For example, both buyer and seller might prefer a two-year contract to sell 100,000 pieces annually at $40 each to a one-year contract at $45 each. The buyer locks in $48 million in revenue and the seller get the pieces at a lower price.

Terminal Game

n. A negotiation strategy designed to exploit your opponent when you are in a high-leverage position. It requires taking your opponent through the five stages of grief (Denial, Anger, Bargaining, Depression, Acceptance) to maximize your return.

Example: A prosecutor has damning evidence against a suspect, so the suspect's BATNA is a long jail sentence. The prosecutor demands the suspect squeal on his partners, then maintains that position until the suspect realizes he has no good options, and agrees to talk.

Bulldog Insight: The Terminal Game can be very effective when you have high leverage. It will damage relationships and should not be used where a continuing relationship is desired. The Terminal Game is described in detail in *The Bulldog Guide to Dealmaking.*

Tit-For-Tat

n. This is the negotiating strategy of responding to an action with a similar action. If they're cooperative, you respond as cooperative. If they are uncooperative, you respond the same way.

Example: A seller offers a discount, then the buyer responds by narrowing the gap. Then the seller refuses to move more and the buyer declares a standoff. The seller must now decide whether to cooperate or lose the deal.

Bulldog Insight: Tit-for Tat is a very effective negotiating strategy. It keeps the negotiation going and leads to strong results. To be effective, you must stick to the strategy, because you are training your opponent. He will eventually learn to be cooperative, because he learns that uncooperative actions will be counterproductive.

Urgency

n. Creating a sense of time pressure to prompt quicker decision-making from the other party. These tactics motivate the other side to act quickly, usually to secure a deal or push for a final decision.

Example: Sammy Seller states clearly, "This offer is only valid until midnight tonight," to create a sense of urgency and push Bob Buyer to make a decision.

Bulldog Insight: Urgency tactics can effectively drive quick action and close deals. Overusing urgency can cause the other party to feel manipulated, potentially damaging the relationship. It's essential to ensure the urgency is genuine to maintain trust and avoid negative repercussions.

Like its cousin, Scarcity, Urgency tactics should never be used in a bluff. If you get called out, you will lose the deal or go crawling back at less value for you.

Walkaway Number

n. This is the minimum acceptable outcome for a negotiator, below which they will not agree to the deal. It's that parties end of the Deal Range.

Example: Larry Landlord is looking for another house to rent to students. He has decided that he will pay no more $400,000 for Charlie Chiseler's house. After much negotiating, Charlie makes a final proposal to sell for $405,000, telling Larry to take it or leave it. Larry walks away.

Bulldog Insight: Your walkaway number serves as a safeguard against unfavorable agreements. It's crucial to identify this number before negotiations begin to avoid emotional decisions. If you're convinced they will not get to this number, make sure you walk away.

Termination Clause

n. Describes how the contract may end early and the notice or cure procedures required.

Example: Either Party may terminate this Agreement at any time, for any reason or no reason, by providing the other Party with thirty (30) days' prior written notice. Either Party may also terminate this Agreement immediately upon written notice if the other Party:

(a) materially breaches any provision of this Agreement and fails to cure such breach within fifteen (15) days after receiving written notice thereof; or

(b) becomes insolvent, files for bankruptcy, or ceases to conduct business in the ordinary course.

Bulldog Insight: A termination clause defines how the relationship ends, including who can walk away, under what circumstances, how much notice is required, and what obligations survive afterward. The clause should clearly state what each side owes (or forfeits) when the contract ends. During negotiations, think through the different events that might cause you and your opponent to want to leave the relationship. Make sure all your concerns are covered.

Waiver Clause

n. Clarifies that not enforcing a right once does not waive the right in the future.

Example: No failure or delay by either Party in exercising any right, power, or privilege under this Agreement shall operate as a waiver thereof, nor shall any single or partial exercise of any such right, power, or privilege preclude any other or further exercise thereof or the exercise of any other right, power, or privilege.

Any waiver of a provision of this Agreement shall be effective only if made in writing and signed by the Party against whom the waiver is sought to be enforced.

Bulldog Insight: The Waiver Clause allows you to give your opponent some flexibility under the contract without giving up the whole deal. Just because you accept a payment that is a week late does not mean you have changed the due date on future payments. Include this clause in all important contracts unless you have a clear reason not to include it.

Win-Win Negotiation

n. A negotiation strategy that focuses on achieving a mutually beneficial outcome where both parties are satisfied with the result. Both parties seek to grow the pie so that more value is created for both sides.

Example: Two NFL General Managers are negotiating a trade. The Vikings have more quality linebackers than they need but are looking for a tight end. The Steelers have more quality tight ends than they need but are looking for a linebacker. Trading a linebacker for a tight end makes both teams better.

Bulldog Insight: The Win-Win strategy requires an understanding of both parties' interests and priorities. The parties will exchange items that are of high value to the other side but low value to them. Look hard to find ways to increase value for both sides.

Zero-Sum Game

n. A negotiation situation where one party benefits only at the expense of the other. One side's gain always equals the other side's loss.

Example: Paul Prom is at a flea market haggling over the price of a used tuxedo and the asking price is $50.00. Any discount Fred Fleamarket gives Paul comes out of his own pocket. If Paul buys it for $35.00, he's gained $15.00 at Fred's expense, perhaps enough to buy some used cufflinks at the next stall.

Bulldog Insight: Zero-sum games require a competitive strategy. To succeed, you must understand everyone's BATNA. If the tuxedo seller has a weak BATNA (it's raining and the flea market is slow) Paul can be aggressive. In fact, very few games are truly zero-sum. When not happy with a Zero Sum game, Bulldogs will change the paradigm by looking for ways to add players or value to make it a Win-Win game.

About the Author

Bring Your Bulldog

Terry Moore earned his reputation as a "Bulldog Lawyer" by being aggressive, tenacious, and practical. He has successfully taken on major league adversaries including Big Oil, Big Pharma, and Big Government. Over the past 40 years, he has won more than $150 million in value for his clients. He's the author of three books: *Big Force Negotiation, The Bulldog Guide to Business Divorce,* and *The Bulldog Guide to Dealmaking.*

Terry advises business clients in a variety of sectors, with concentrations in sports and entertainment, oilfield services, media, and health care. He's especially good at handling business partner disputes and litigation. He is recognized by Best Lawyers in America, Litigation Council of America, and Superlawyers, among others.

He has owned and operated successful radio properties, a professional hockey league, and a real estate investment company. This unique experience, in both law and business, gives him the specialized skills to solve disruptive business problems, from litigation to transactions to multi-party workouts.

Licensed to practice in Minnesota, North Dakota and South Dakota, Terry is also a popular speaker and seminar leader on business and legal topics.

If you have concerns about negotiations we can help.

If you have questions or would like to arrange for Terry to speak to your group, contact him directly at 612-396-5588.

Terrance W. Moore, Esq.
Helmuth & Johnson
8050 W 78th Street
Edina, MN 55439
www.TheBulldogGuides.com
TMoore@HJLawFirm.com

Made in the USA
Monee, IL
04 November 2026

67387556R00056